C000179079

Gallery Books
Editor: Peter Fallon

OTHER PEOPLE'S HOUSES

Vona Groarke

OTHER PEOPLE'S HOUSES

Gallery Books

Other People's Houses
is first published
simultaneously in paperback
and in a clothbound edition
on 29 April 1999.

The Gallery Press
Loughcrew
Oldcastle
County Meath
Ireland

*All rights reserved. For permission
to reprint or broadcast these poems
write to The Gallery Press.*

© Vona Groarke 1999

ISBN 1 85235 240 X (*paperback*)
       1 85235 241 8 (*clothbound*)

The Gallery Press acknowledges the financial assistance
of An Chomhairle Ealaíon / The Arts Council, Ireland,
and the Arts Council of Northern Ireland.

Contents

for Tommy and Eve,
homebirds

One need not be a chamber to be haunted,
one need not be a house.
— Emily Dickinson, 'Ghosts'

Indoors

It breaks apart as water will not do
when I pull, hard, away from me,
the corners bunched in my two hands
to steer a true and regulated course.

I plunge the needle through and through,
dipping, tacking, coming up again.
The ripple of thread that follows pins,
out of its depth, a shallow hem.

I smooth the waves and calm the folds.
Then, to ensure an even flow,
I cast a line which runs from hook to hook
and pulls the net in overlapping pleats.

Which brings me to the point where I am
hanging a lake, by one shore, in my room,
to swell and billow between the light
and opaque, unruffled dark.

I step in. The room closes round me
and scarcely puckers when I move my limbs.
I step out. The path is darkened where I walk,
my shadow steaming off in all this sun.

House Rules

The foundation is the opening gambit;
what's added are storeys or rooms. But
its premise is the open ground, unbuilt.

❖

The walls are true, impregnable and straight.
They break the rain, contain the family fight,
cleave what's outside in, and inside out.

❖

Windows are transparent, yet what surfaces
is not the beds, the books, or fireplace,
but sunken eyes, the stranger's dour face.

❖

The doors are points of entry and deliverance.
They are obliged to look both ways at once
and to admit, or to refuse, the difference.

❖

The floors uphold the building of the house
and, while supportive, may also raze
its aspirations. Subversively, of course.

❖

The roof straddles the house.
Yet for all its confinement and poise,
it is, in turn, preoccupied with skies.

House Contents

In the disco of a town hotel
boxes are numbered and packed
according to the condition
of their random artefacts.

Wedding gifts from the '30s,
souvenirs from children's trips,
a gilt-framed oil, an inlaid chair,
cut glass and china (chipped).

Objects without purpose,
details adrift from plot:
the piano and piano stool
for sale in separate lots.

House Viewing

Though you try to keep your voices to a hush
you can hear her cough and fidget in the back
when he tells you, 'I don't think this one's for us'.
You don't want to be unkind and something —
the lack of photos, all the single beds,
the spit and bristle of the small gas fire,
the tins of sardines heaped up on the shelf? —
has made you want to cry, or very near.
When you leave and head down for the bus
the same thing makes you kiss his hand
and say out of the blue, 'You know I love you'.
And imagine all the way back into town
the years together, deep as Turkish rugs,
your home together, bright as gold milk-jugs.

When she saw you she thought, 'It won't be them'.
Something about his damson-coloured shirt
and your briefcase just wouldn't suit
the beauty board, the hall's green lino tiles.
She waited while you fidgetted upstairs,
your silly whispers tumbling down the hall,
and didn't even smile when he took her hand
and gave the usual, 'Well, thanks very much.
It's really beautiful. We'll be back in touch.'
When you were gone, she put the photos back,
re-set the central heating, fed the cat,
and put her feet up on the draylon pouffe,
imagining her donkey-brown settee
in the front room of her daughter's semi-d.

House Plan

A landscaped garden, a façade and a drive,
some client's notion of the ideal place to live,
have been composed into a scheme of rooms
and set off with unnecessary trims,
prompting words like 'classical' or 'fine'
as delicate responses to such adequate design.
For purposes of scale, a figure has been drawn
on the blackened square at the back marked LAWN.
With this casual shading, it's difficult to see
if the face above the stick-arms seems to be
that of a proud owner, or an occasional guest
taking the air between sundown and breakfast.
Or a villager who, on passing the empty house,
has slipped in to choose an overflowing rose.

Open House

At first glance every house looks much the same
as the others adjoining and sharing the name
of Sycamore Court (though there's barely a tree
to be seen and there's certainly no royalty).
Instead we have seventy-six ideal homes
laid out with the stature of so many tombs
in seven straight lines that all run parallel
concluding in debris that doesn't bode well
for the 'intimate setting' or 'rural surrounds'
suggestive to buyers of huge estate grounds.
At least when I viewed the plans for Number 6
I saw something more than just mortar and bricks:
I saw myself, permanent, rooted at last,
with all the aplomb of the propertied class;
I saw myself sacrosanct, safe and secure
inside the enclosure of my own front door,
my neighbour and I quite distinct from each other
blissfully unconcerned with all the bother
of civil exchanges and how-do-you-do's
that are the first step, as everyone knows,
to cars in your drive and complaints about noise,
to cameras and telescopes trained on your house,
to asides about guests who have clearly slept over,
suggestions about how to deal with your lover,
and comments about how your clothes really sit
so neatly now that you've been getting fit.
Moreoever I'd swear that I've recently seen
my neighbour from two up at my Wheelie Bin
looking like somebody looking for clues
to my personal hygiene or liking for booze.
Which he'll probably share with the woman who's out
adjusting her garden from morning to night.
Or the man who accepted his wife's nomination
as Chair of the Residents' Association
which, needless to say, is an onerous duty

that needs dedication, and so he must duly
jot down all the numbers of visiting cars
and bring the lists weekly on up to the guards
to ascertain if that jeep parked at my fence
might harbour a convict of evil intent.
Or if my new boyfriend whom he called a *pup*
when he got the two fingers should be locked up.
This neighbourly interface is all forestalled
by the containing gesture of four straight walls
that keeps me safely in and them safely out
save for a rousing, occasional shout
that I won't really mind if it won't really last,
that I'll probably eavesdrop with my drinking glass
pressed up to the wall and my casual ear,
only listening to what they don't mind if I hear.
It's only breeze blocks, plaster, paint, insulation
that maintain this illusion of neat isolation,
but how can we really be quite so distinct
when the smell of my own bin advances the stink
of next door's, and the same weeds, regardless of source
will choke all our flowers with impartial force?
And it's not just a network of pipes that connects us
with life's deeper purpose: we're joined in a nexus
that overrides each individual claim
to freedom, uniting in one lofty aim
all for one, one for all (unless it applies
to my ride-on mower, my new set of pliers).
And, in theory, I'm perfectly keen to subscribe
to the notion of residents being a tribe
with certain shared interests and some common ground.
But must the subscription be two hundred pounds?
All of which keeps me up, calculating and mean,
imagining bedrooms which I've never seen
with layouts that probably look just like mine
with too little space, too much country pine.

But even allowing for different tastes
as to where the master bed ought to be placed
along with the lockers and pink wicker chair,
I still can imagine that my bed will share
a similar setting, against the same wall
as the bed of the stranger I should one day call
to ask if he has been receiving my post
though doubtless he'll tell me to go and get . . . lost.
Now here we are, just as close as two ticks
who've been separated by one course of bricks
and the fact that my feet both point to the west
while his are in line with his ultimate rest.
Other than that, I could almost reach over
to tussle his hair or to pull back the cover.
But the distance between us may never be breached
and my sleeping partner may never be reached
unless, by an accident or design flaw,
the wall that divides us should crumble and fall,
or else be rolled back by the great hand of fate
as happened to Lazarus, or the guests on *Blind Date*.
So that we might meet for the very first time
unsurprised by the question of *Your place or mine?*

Folderol

I have been walking by the harbour
where I see it's recently sprayed
that *Fred loves Freda*, and *Freda cops Fred*.
Which reminds me of you, and the twenty-four

words for 'nonsense' I wrote on your thighs and back
(the night you came home from her house with some cock-
and-bull story of missed connections and loose ends)
with passion-fruit lipstick and mascara pens.

Including, for the record: blather, drivel, trash,
prattle, palaver, waffle, balderdash, gibberish, shit.
Thinking I had made a point of sorts, but not
so sure when I woke up to find my own flesh

covered with your smudged disgrace
while you, of course, had vanished without trace.

Two Storey

Take just the kind of argument where she ends up
  in the bedroom
slapping the pillow against the wall, while he festers
  in the yard
kicking pebbles within inches of the glass. It consumes
  the house
which begs the question: Where will they find room
  to make it up?

Will a heady conference in the small hours push them,
  come morning,
to their separate beds, resentment settled round them
  like stale air?
Or, reconciled, will they breakfast together in muted tones,
  dividing
rooms into 'His' and 'Hers' in yet another equitable
  housework plan?

House-bound

The blind holds it in check. As you let it down
it tightens its grip on an evening otherwise unstirred.
What you see is a calculated hour which he is likely
to tie up in a darkened, half-dark upstairs room.

What he brings with him is another world. When,
with your loose fingers, you undo him, then its
refuse, its fog, its chips and cigarettes rub off on you.
You can almost memorize it with your tongue.

He brings you messages. You take him at his word
and once a week allow him in. He thinks of missionaries,
the bond that never breaks. Not that it matters.
It's not company you're keeping, but your hand in.

The skein of darkness in his hands is another story.
He is tightening it all night, so that the stars you keep
initially at bay bear down and perforate your darker sky.
Inside of which you lie, and take it as it comes.

It should mean silence, but it never does. The unused
words thicken in your head, the room, your open door,
the road going out of town. Something like
'Good evening'. 'A great stretch.' 'How do you do?'

You think it is a double bind: on one hand, there's the dark
he lays you in; on the other, there's the chance that he might
mean the world to you. That one day, you may wake alone to
a shift of crumpled fields, a room released to light, an easy life.

The House of Hair

It used to be a house of ill-repute.
She said she still got calls at wayward hours
from gentlemen not looking for a trim.

She was quick and supple and made-up.
The punters liked her, she had good hands
and a braided rope tattoo on her inner arm.

She'd dab her wrists with musk after each one.
It drew the room around her fingertips,
the turn of her breasts, her thighs, her shallow hips.

And I, waiting my turn, would watch them
close their eyes as she'd finish them off
by brushing down the last hairs from each chin.

She cut my hair up short and gave it back
with numbers for two wig-makers in town.
I found it three years later, in a drawer

when it had loosened out and strayed
to fill the bag with soft, dark fur
that didn't smell of me, but of her skin.

House Guest

He said: 'Yes, thank you. Very well indeed.'
I believed him until I stripped the bed
of the negative impression he had made
in sleep as fraught as most of what he said.

Last night he praised the food and our good taste
and duly ate too loudly and too fast.
Last night he waved his hand before his face
and said, 'OK. I think what you mean is . . . '

The Dream House

Downstairs is all civility and grace.
The rooms proceed with well-intentioned flow
that takes in practicality and show.
Everything is in its ordained place.

The clock predicts familiar time.
The chairs are settled where they always were.
The chimney is untroubled by a fire,
and nothing stirs for any move of mine.

I am following my guide, as I must do,
in silence, while he talks me through the plan.
I am ushered in, informed, and then moved on
through lower rooms in a house I do not know.

We round back on the hall. I know it now —
the difficult stairs, the family oils
arranged in staggered time along the walls,
the faces that refuse my wary eye.

As we ascend, something seems to change.
The mood of certainty falters. There's a mirror
in which I am caught, for a moment, somewhere
between surprise and reassurance. I look strange.

He gives me fewer facts; he grows more quiet.
I begin to see for myself. The doors are ajar.
I choose the nearest and notice that the curtains are
the colour of my eyes. In certain light.

He opens the wardrobe. I see clothes that I might wear;
shoes in my size in a row under the bed.
On the shelf, some books that I would like to read —
and when I look behind me, a closed door.

The house is all beyond me; the room recedes.
I begin to lose the sense of what I saw.
In all this detail, one apparent flaw:
my unlost earring crumpled on the sheets.

House Wine

It's not the way you raise it to your mouth
or hold the glass against the linen cloth
or pass it gingerly beneath your snout
or sip it with your lips and eyebrows wrought.

It's not the way you ask for the *new* list
or keep on about the year you almost guessed.
It's not even that you never buy the best
or that sometimes I might just want to get pissed.

It's not about the kind of words you choose,
the dusty terms, the latest-learned French phrase,
the silly adjectives that want to make no sense,
the loaded *Mmm* that hints more than it says.

It's the way you click your full glass against mine
and always say: *There's poetry, but here's wine.*

Domestic Arrangements

1 THE HALL

Where the world is introduced
as a play of light which scans
an abstract strategy from which
the house derives its plans.

Here a door admits the presence
of undistinguished air
to a set of rooms established as
a various elsewhere.

2 THE SITTING ROOM

Where the best intentions
are displaced and settled
in the fittings and décor.
Fire and an easy chair,

paintings, rows of books,
cultivate an earnestness
confounded by the overlooked
omission of a door.

3 THE LIBRARY

The accumulated wisdom of
someone's ancient family line
and the contents of two bookshops,
antiquarian, since closed down.

Books by the yard, leather-bound,
suggesting intellect and wit
except around doors and windows
where they've been trimmed to fit.

4 THE STUDY

Where business is done on deckle
embossed with the name of the house.
Where bills and accounts are juggled
to fix a balance of profit and loss.

Where excess is indicated by
the respect the room commands:
the Chesterfield, the mahogany desk,
and a wealth of final demands.

5 THE BREAKFAST ROOM

From which an aspect over lawns
and a carefully managed view
of parterres and a lily pond
replete with morning dew

detract from the vision incarnate
that packs into a fleshy yawn
wrinkles, bald spot, bloodshot eyes
and gaping dressing gown.

6 THE DINING ROOM

A conversation piece
where selected features like
a bas relief or urn inspire
and accommodate high talk.

Where appreciated mouthfuls
are served, then come and go
to tasteful strains of Satchmo
or Astrud Gilberto.

7 THE KITCHEN

Dreams of concealment,
of explaining clean away
such functionary details
as the everyday.

Provisions must be made for
polished surfaces and glass.
Amongst the labelled storage jars
ferments a kind of chaos.

8 THE PANTRY

Ought to be lined with alabaster
and white marble tiles, or some
imperishable material to withstand
calamity or what-may-come.

Its illustrative foresight
should be a quiet rebuke
to the instinctive, as in the eponymous
painting by Pieter de Hooch.

9 THE CONSERVATORY

Where future daughters of the house
will languish and endure
the promise of orchids:
cultivated, but impure.

The glass obscured by rubber plants,
the heat at any hour
supply ideal conditions
to graft, or to deflower.

10 THE MASTER BEDROOM

Where architecture can't conceive
of territories staked out
and subsequently bargained
in some secondary plot.

Where plans don't always focus
on an ideal physical form
and the consummation of desire
is not, perhaps, a room.

11 THE BATHROOM

Alludes to the natural world
as a sylvan spree
of tiled peacocks, willows
and classical statuary

elevating baser moments
and positioned to dismiss
the theory of mortality,
the deathly hit and miss.

12 THE SECOND BEDROOM

Built with the stuff of dreams
and required to withstand
ghosts, hobgoblins and (hardest of all)
the Invisible Man.

Child's play. Brick upon brick:
all come tumbling down,
but safe as houses later
with darkness strewn around.

13 THE GUEST BEDROOM

Packed under the overhead tank
but not lavish with its space,
adequate, but not designed
to encourage lengthy stays.

Exhibits an ostensible taste,
soft towels and subtleties.
On the bedside table
a *Guide to Local B&Bs*.

14 THE ATTIC

Between tea-chests and boxes
a strange assemblage lurks
of portraits and mad relatives
and gadgets that don't work.

As nature abhors a vacuum,
it follows that beneath
the roof, suppressed desire
should accumulate, as heat.

The Lighthouse

I heard her tell the story another way.
She set it, not in the village, where
the parish priest was telling the crowd
about light in the darkness
and the dawn of a new age —

she set it in the kitchen of their house,
with three women resting
and the day's work done. She told it
so we would listen for the music
of the room when it was still:

the rustle of the fire in the grate;
the single held note of a teaspoon
from which the knitting needles took their cue;
the steady flutter of the carriage clock
that kept their breath in check.

One of them might sleep and her nodding glasses
snag the firelight and scatter it
around the room to return in the more
familiar shine of cups on the dresser,
copper pans, her sister's wedding-band.

In the village, a crowd of overcoated men
sent up a cheer for progress and prosperity
for all . . .
            And in the length of time
it took to turn a switch and to make light
of their house, three women saw themselves

stranded in a room that was nothing like
their own, with pockmarked walls
and ceiling stains, its cobwebs and its grime:
their house undone and silenced
by the clamour of new light.

Lighthouses

Houses in darkness are few and far between.
We are driving home cross-country as the year
is drawing in. Rooms are turning towards us
as we pass. Such rooms, set out as wedding gifts,
all confidence and shine. Living rooms with lamps
and stoked-up fires; mirrors above them that catch
a glimpse of us; windows flecked with Christmas trees
and flicking bulbs that are telling us
to notice this . . . Don't notice this. Drive on.

House Fire

Lately, a fire in the car park that sparked loose talk of bombs and broken faith. In the morning, it got out. After her death, they had burned her caravan, fittings, furniture, the lot.

The fire took care of her worldly remains: a place at a table, a side of the bed, a way of resting her hands beside the sink. The fire was to silence whatever might call her back. The fire was supposed to set her free.

One day there was a camp of them spilling out like rainwater stopped in saucepans on the footpath and the bonnets of half-broken cars. Then they were gone, moved on.

In their wake, a ring of blackened saplings, indelible shadows on the lock-up wall, the tarmac scorched for good. And a shattered hull that still rests in the dead end of the old car park.

No one will touch it: the usual scrappers won't go nigh or near. The winos and the skangers keep well off. No cars park around it, shoppers circle it. The Council says its hands are tied.

There's talk of a strange whistling sound, a blue light in the dead of night. Someone swears her dog, or someone's, has been left behind. It is taking on a life of its own.

They won't come back this way. What's done is done. And if the sagging roof and shattered glass mean anything, it is not to do with her, who kept her windows netted and intact.

Workhouses

One was a factory that never thrived
but still, above the door, retains the sign —
the company name it never was known by.

One was a nursing home old people feared.
When someone died, the nuns ensured
the shroud and rosary beads, the cheapest box.

One was burned, the fire watched for miles
from windows that took up the blaze
and carried it, like fever, house to house.

One was stripped of timber, brick and stone.
What remained, when it had been picked over,
were bare-boned rooms, identical, bereft.

One gradually capsized, until the earth
closed over it, fresh grass undid
its sunken rooms, its barely buried roof.

One has been untouched for years,
its door undarkened, its air unmoved,
the field around it never ploughed in Spring.

The Big House

I took it for another ancient ruin
with gaping windows and the roof all in.
But as we drove up underneath its bulk
I saw that what was darkening our truck
was not the shadow of a burnt-out pile
but a stack of tightly-packed hay-bales
built up like bricks, its façade high
and monumental, latticed to the sky.

Around the Houses

'Oh no,' she said, 'you're wrong. Underwood
never came here. And if someone did

write about the ratio of internal
to external air around the vernacular

houses of Irishtown, Ballinadrum,
I'm sure it could not have been him.

For everyone knows he turned off in Clogher
and never made it this far.'

The Courthouse

One day a month, it becomes a kind of fortress
besieged by lads with haircuts and new ties
shifting between their cigarettes and briefs —
men of letters sprawled on granite walls
wherein a flurry of vowels and balding wigs
is thick around the pillars and closed doors.
On other days, the silence is upheld:
no one breathes a word; new light is thrown,
unnoticed; a damp patch slurs;
the windows, in their cases, rattle on.

The Sandcastle

We spent ages making it impregnable and fast,
a crenellated keep complete with flag
and drawbridge, moat and blind portcullis.

And ages later, talking our way past
to gold and silver, torches and intrigues,
dark rumours gaining ground outside the walls.

Holiday Home

Pre-fabricated, four rooms and a view
of haycocks and white horses on the bay.
Deckchairs slumped into the flattened grass
edged with vetch and shards of broken glass.
A bed-settee, a fridge in the living room,
the angelus and tea's old news and *Spam*.
Towels that never dried, togs on the wall,
three swims a day, hair always thick with salt.
Trips to the village for water, milk and gin,
and scampi in the hotel now and then.
Bunk beds, one wardrobe, lino on the floors,
rusted window-locks and swollen doors.
Rough rods for fishing mackerel off the rocks,
the *Naomh Éanna,* watched for, twice a day, for luck.
Last year's novels, dog-eared on the shelf,
late games of whist, gin-rummy, twenty-five.
My father, stepping out to lock the car,
humming lines from one of his four airs:
'Galway Bay'; 'I'll Take You Home Again, Kathleen';
'The Mountains of Mourne'; 'When You Were Sweet Sixteen'.
Us listening inside for notes that swayed and fell
in shadows on the back of Weavers' Hill
behind the house, where these days petered out,
like spray thrown up by neighbours' dipped headlights
or rain astray on bracken, heather, gorse;
the journey back inland behind his hearse,
sand in my sandals, his runners in the boot
with shorts and T-shirts, him in his good suit.

Nearer Home

My father is standing outside the front door,
pointing out to me the Plough and North Star.
He says, 'Look up, child, just as far as you can.'
I see freckles join up on the back of his hand.

The Slaughterhouse

Some gap in the sidings, a man too few
at the turn into the pens, and they were out,
scattering like buckshot through the cars.
Until a clutch of lads in bloodied aprons
bore down on them with shouts and whirring arms.
Within minutes, they were gathered,
it was done. The lads strayed back to work,
the steel doors closed on the skirl and din,
the driver tidied his gates, and pulled away.

It was chill to the bone. I had been called to come.
I was late, though I didn't know then, not on the journey,
with the plain-chant of the train seeing me home
through towns that came too slowly,
like final words, like beads in her hands;
not when I passed within miles of the house;
not at the station; not as I watched
the flurry of pigs; not when they were bested;
not while they were killed; not when I was driven away.

House Style

When my grandmother looked into my mother's eyes
she saw what I see in my daughter's.

The Play House

The table's underside is solid ground,
their boots across it have somewhere to go.
The torch is a streetlamp encouraging intrigue —
there are whispers, smothered words and drawn-out plans.
They are lying on the floor with their legs stretched up.
Eve's hair has settled like a wide-brimmed hat
and Tom is making secrets with his hands.
They have the whole world to themselves
under cover of darkness that hangs,
like woollen blankets, down each side.
Their steps are heavy and together to begin with,
then loosen out and gradually fall off.

The Glasshouse

It started with lapis lazuli,
an uncut nugget of blue-veined grey
that was your first gift to me.

Since then we have marked time or
love with stones like agate, quartz and amber,
which are, for us, just one way to remember.

For ten years, husband, we've been piling stones
and shifting them, in weighty bags, from one
place to another, and then home

to a house we wished on the lines of *amour
courtois* or happenstance, or some more
improbable stuff than bricks and mortar.

When we had nothing to speak of, we used stone.
Now that our house is set to dwell upon
a solid, shored-up bedrock of its own,

we think of it as bulk and not detail.
So what chance now for our bag of polished shale
to be turned out and worked into a trail

that would take us from our first word
to our last, if it has been said or heard,
in the here and now of language almost shared?

I could say that one is glazed with rain
the way your hand was when you wrote your name
and number in my book that Saturday.

Or that one has the smoothness of your cheek,
that one is dimpled like the small of your back,
or that one is freckled like your sunburned neck.

I could say that there is one which is warm,
as though you had been holding it in the palm
of your hand, a while before I came;

that one is perfect as the white of your eye,
and that there is one which I think may
just remind you, afterwards, of me;

that the hilt of one could hurt us,
or pierce the walls of a delicate house
that, in the end, may be as breakable as glass.

But it cannot slip from your hand or
from my own, my love, not now, when our
stones that we picked in time are thrown asunder

on Ballagan Point, where we stood lately, side by side
with stones in our pockets and stones in our hands,
to promise each other the sky, and its blue-veined clouds.

The Image of the House

The exact measure of it is a square-cut house
whose sealed approaches and steel-glazed panes
brook no disturbance in an accomplished scene.

Or a roof pitched past the picture-frame
as squat garden walls indicate a meeting point
somewhere between the rear and god-knows-where.

Infinity suggested by a white plastered wall
that leads the eye beyond attendant trees
to intimate the sky — a world elsewhere.

Without. Where I stand with my small son
face-on to the closed front door which all the while
receives us, takes us in. When he lifts his fist

against it, it may be to announce that we are here
or, failing that, to adjust the one flaw in the replete glass
which is his hand, which is our presence, us.

The Empty House

When we are gone, the house will close over us
as though we'd been swimmers in an unmoved sea.
The cisterns will unruffle, the fridge will wheeze on,
and the shape we made in the bed will pucker out.

The house will replace us with sounds of its own:
the shuffle of pages as we pull the door hard,
the phone ringing out, the occasional clock,
and only the letterbox will break the settled air.

All these shadows from the beech tree in the back
that close on my arm as I reach to turn the key
will swell with a glitter that will take in the room
and, this evening, drain what is left of us away.

Other People's Houses

for Conor

Last night I walked to a house where we
once lived. It's not looking good.
There's been a fire and the roof's caved in.
The garden's scotched with grass and weeds
and most of the windows are through.

The ceiling of the sitting room is upended
on the floor. No trace now of the yellow
couch that was our 'amour prop',
or the stack of romantic novels you had me
stand up on to save your aching back.

Or the radio we lived by in those days,
you with your cricket and creaky plays
on the BBC; me with my news on the
hour, every hour, lest something
outside of us should ever change.

Or the soggy mattress where we sailed
beyond the beyonds and, somehow,
back again to wake each morning
to the blue of our eyes and the three
mile trek for newspapers and milk.

Or the porch where I used to write those
flowery poems before I knew you so well,
halfway between the In- and Outdoors,
where one time, looking two ways at once,
I saw you stranded in both, and thought

I would throw in my lot with yours.
Which is about it. We lived in
other people's houses then. Now,
we have a stake in a place of our own
which keeps us steady and tied.

I want you to know, not that nothing
is lost — even I could not promise
so much — but that something remains,
here, even after so many years:
the starlings are still nesting in the eaves.

And last night as I watched them
their circular orbit put me in mind
of the rhumba you danced with a bumble-bee
right there at the gate, on the day that we left
this house behind us, together and for good.

Outdoors

It happens so easily. We've been watching trees
gather shadow on the wall, on the lookout
for a moment when we might call it a day
and settle for the night. But only our room
is losing ground, while nothing outside is lost.

In the time it takes for him to turn to meet my eye
we have missed it; it has happened without us again.
I give in, put on the light, and watch for him to be
stranded, confronting me from the garden, his back
to me in the kitchen, his eyes, in the glass, on me.

What does it matter that we have made a home
where we can draw the curtains and talk of tomorrow,
if we are thinking of this: the shapes we made in darkness,
our kitchen at sea on the lawn, our table set out
in the branches, our faces marooned in stars?

The Haunted House

Think of rooms threaded by voices. Think of home:
the typewriter chipping away at the small hours;
a stack of ancient newspapers and the scissors
surely blunted by this time. 'Think of home.'

As though you could step in and find them
waiting for you with your tea kept warm.
As though I could keep one hand on the lock
and the other on the handle of the door.

Either way, there's a headless doll that will
never be found under a tree in the yard.
There's a thin voice singing 'I dreamt I dwelt'
and a stream in a ditch where the house dips in

that has my face in it. The time is now,
and I never will step into this house again.

Acknowledgements

Acknowledgements are due to the editors of the following publications where these poems, or versions of them, have appeared: *Chapman, The Irish Review, The Irish Times, Metre, The North, Poetry Ireland Review, P.N. Review, R.O.P.E.S., The Sunday Times, Tabla, Thumbscrew* and *Verse.*

The author gratefully acknowledges receipt of a Bursary in Literature from An Chomhairle Ealaíon / The Arts Council, Ireland, in 1996.

Thanks are also due to the Rooney Prize Foundation for a Residence Bursary in 1996, and to the staff of the Tyrone Guthrie Centre, Annaghmakerrig, where several of these poems were written.